The *Great* Israel Scavenger Hunt

Teacher's Lesson Plan Manual

By Sharon D. Halper

24 Ready-to-Use Lesson Plans

Includes Experiential Learning activities and ways to use the Internet to bring Israel to life in your classroom.

Project Editor: Judith Sandman
Design: Jill A. Winitzer

Springfield, New Jersey
ISBN: 978-0-87441-930-6 • Manufactured in the United States of America

Behrman House, Inc.
www.behrmanhouse.com

CONTENTS

INTRODUCTION

The Great Israel Scavenger Hunt invites students in grades 2 and 3 to tour the Land of Israel with Daniel and his Israeli cousin, Rivkah. Rivkah and Daniel uncover clues about seven special objects. As students move through each chapter, they participate in the scavenger hunt, too, uncovering clues and earning stickers at the end of each adventure.

Traveling the land, they become familiar with the geography and topography of Israel, as well as its major cities and sites. The connection of the Jewish people to the land throughout history, as well as the vibrancy of modern Israeli life, are emphasized throughout.

There are eight chapters in *The Great Israel Scavenger Hunt:* an introductory chapter, a concluding return home, and one chapter for each of the major cities/areas of Israel—Haifa, the Galilee, Tel Aviv, Jerusalem, the Judean Desert and Negev, and Eilat.

The Great Israel Scavenger Hunt includes these features:

- **Israel Locator,** which highlights the area to which students are traveling in each chapter.
- A **Clue** to the word that will be revealed at each **Scavenger Hunt Sticker Stop,** an opportunity for students to use what they have learned to earn a sticker to add to the two-page map of Israel on pages 14-15 of the textbook.
- An **Israel Fun Fact** that provides interesting information about the location.
- **A Window to Israel**, giving students a chance to see the application of their learning to modern Israeli life.
- Photographs that capture the essence of the area, as well as interactive formats that allow students to personalize their learning.

STRUCTURE OF THIS LESSON PLAN MANUAL

This Lesson Plan Manual presents 24 ready-to-use lesson plans of approximately 50 minutes each for *The Great Israel Scavenger Hunt*. It includes suggestions for teaching every element of the student text. In addition, suggestions for the use of technology and ideas for family engagement are offered in several lessons.

Each chapter in this manual corresponds to a chapter in the textbook and includes the following elements:

- **Essential Question** An overarching question that reflects the main idea of the lesson.
- **Lesson Objectives** Goals for students to achieve by the end of the lesson.
- **Getting Started** A set induction to get students thinking about their own lives as a vehicle for the ideas they will learn in the lesson.
- **Exploring the Text** A step-by-step guide for presenting the lesson, including suggested questions and activities, and the approximate time for each segment of the lesson.
- **Experiential Learning** An opportunity for students to take their learning off the page and into their hands.
- **Wrapping It Up** A short activity to discuss, or review and reflect on, the main ideas presented in the lesson.
- **The Tech Connection** Ideas for online materials and digital applications to enhance selected lessons.

Using This Lesson Plan Manual

As you begin to plan your year, determine when you will teach each chapter. The 24 lessons in the manual will help you to make Israel a year-long reality for your students.

Before you begin to teach each textbook chapter, read the Lesson Plan Manual to familiarize yourself with the essential questions and activities designed to accompany each chapter. Lessons may be used as written or adapted to suit your students, schedule, supplies, and space. In adapting a lesson, consider its essential question, and be certain that your adaptations are equipping students to respond to it. In some cases you may decide to alter the essential question. Be certain that the activities lead to responses to the question.

The manual is easy to use with the student text. All references to maps, photographs, and readings are in bold, followed by the page number. For example, Lesson 1 of Chapter 1 recommends: "Using the **world map** on pages 10-11, students locate Israel...."

Teaching Strategies

Opening Each Session

1. Help students move from the previous lesson to the new lesson by summarizing the main idea of the earlier lesson and providing a preview of the upcoming one. Will there be similarities or differences between the two? What will be eye-opening, cool, or fun in the new lesson?
2. The opening Lesson Plan for each chapter includes the use of the map on pages 14-15 to trace the trip from the previous chapter to the upcoming lesson. The repeated use of the map will increase students' familiarity with Israel's geography and the names of its major cities and bodies of water.
3. Post the Essential Question for the lesson to be studied on the board. Invite a volunteer to read the Essential Question aloud. Briefly discuss the meaning of the question, making certain that students understand it. You might keep a visual record of previous Essential Questions and refer to them to review responses and enable students to see the development of their learning.
4. That visual record also provides a means of communication with parents. Seeing the Essential Question on the board gives them information on what you've taught each week.

Interpersonal and Intrapersonal Learners

Some students do best when working alone (intrapersonal); others are more successfully engaged when working in a group (interpersonal). This Lesson Plan Manual balances opportunities for working alone, working in pairs or small groups, and working as a class.

Group Work

Many lessons include opportunities for group work. Think ahead about how you will form working groups for each assignment. It is important to vary the composition of your groups. For some tasks, you will want students with a variety of skills and interests. For others, you may choose to group together students with similar skills and interests. Other factors to consider in creating groups: Will you strive to create gender balance? Widen social groups? Balance students from a variety of feeder schools and neighborhoods? Account for dominant and docile personalities? Further friendships that you think are a good match, while avoiding less desirable pairings? What about the student who prefers to work alone? Try to ensure that every student will be successful socially as well as academically when working in groups.

One way to ensure successful outcomes is to be certain that every student understands his or her responsibility within the group. You might consider breaking down the group's assignment so that each student has a specific task.

Reading the Text

In determining how the text will be read, be mindful of students who are aural learners. To best understand the material, they will need to hear the information. You may choose to conduct the lessons so students both follow along and hear the text.

Experiential Learning

If you've ever eaten a hot fudge sundae, you understand the value of experiential learning. We learn from seeing things, we learn from hearing or reading about the experiences of others, but the most impactful learning experience occurs when we do something ourselves.

- Experiential Learning takes the content of each lesson and asks that students analyze it, reflect on it, solve problems, or make decisions based on it. Cognitive content is filtered through the life experiences and personalities of each student as they create, illustrate, play, display, respond, and debate. They take the information from the page and transform the content into a dynamic product.
- Experiential Learning allows students to learn about themselves and one another. Students discover their strengths and develop new ones, and naturally find friends with whom they can work.
- Experiential Learning opportunities enable students to value their successful experiences as well as to respect formal learning. These opportunities create a constructive environment in the class and positive memories for students.
- The prospect of engaging in an active experience leads students to look forward to class.

Experiential Learning enables students to answer the eternal parental question, "What did you do today?" with enthusiasm and meaning.

Student Portfolios

Many of the activities suggested in this Lesson Plan Manual yield student work that can be assembled into individual portfolios. These portfolios can be used as part of teacher-student or teacher-parent conferences. They provide concrete examples of how a student is engaged in the material presented. While many of the suggested projects that are included in this Lesson Plan Manual remain in the classroom, you might choose to make color copies of some of them to include in student portfolios.

Portfolios might be presented at an end-of-year *siyum* to which family members are invited. Students' textbooks and portfolios will be a reminder of your students' year in Israel.

The Tech Connection

Technology offers two paths to enriching your students' learning experiences. One path can bring music, videos, and other digital materials into the classroom; the other path leads home to families.

- To reach into the home, create a Class-to-Home connection with a class website, Wikispace, or newsletter, briefly summarizing activities, website recommendations for home use, photographs of the class "in action," and student comments you might like to share.
- Parents become partners in Jewish learning when given the tools to do so. Use the web connection to keep parents updated on Hebrew vocabulary their children are using in school, ideas for adult-level learning that parallels their child's curriculum, and glimpses of classroom activities. Provide conversation starters based on the current lesson and classroom discussion so that parents can be active participants in their child's learning.
- Help your families make Israel real by suggesting exciting websites that you have found, including sources for Israeli products, or news and weather from Israel. Subscribe to a wide variety of e-newsletters on topics related to Israel. Your learning will be current and vibrant, and you will be a valuable source to students and parents alike.
- Technology can enrich the classroom experience with the sights and sounds of Israel. Search engines such as http://www.bing.com/images and http://www.google.com/images can provide maps, pictures, newspapers, advertisements, etc.—all components of Israeli life. Http://www.youtube.com offers links to Israeli music videos, city tours, and features of modern Israeli life. From the *Kotel* to McDonald's, technology can bring living images of Israel into the class.
- Thanks to the availability of clip art and of Hebrew fonts and Hebrew sign maker, teacher-made materials can now look like the work of a professional designer. Search for free clip art intended for educational purposes. Remember to credit sources appropriately. Assigning proper credit is a tenet of Jewish law, it's the civil law, and it provides others with sources that can lead them to valuable materials.

The Family Connection

Parents appreciate the opportunity for meaningful engagement in the life of the class. Invite parents to visit your classroom when they pick up their children and see how their child's vision of Israel is changing and growing. Students might act as one-minute docents, giving parents a taste of the day's class based on student-created materials as part of the lesson just before dismissal.

Ask parents for their participation in specific and time-limited ways. They might share in the preparation of foods or craft materials for a lesson, bring in their own souvenirs or photos of Israel, or provide musical accompaniment to songs that students are learning. Active parent participation lets students see that their parents value Jewish education.

BEING INCLUSIVE

Some of us learn best by listening, some by seeing, and others by doing. The Lesson Plan Manual reflects a variety of learning styles, offering all students opportunities to be successful.

- Emphasize to students the importance of following the text when others are reading. Encourage volunteers reading aloud to do so in a way that is fluent and clear.
- The brevity of the text will allow time for you to emphasize important points, paraphrase the content, and review vocabulary. To maximize student learning, post key words, both Hebrew and English, on a word wall, and define the words each time they are used. Refer back to those words, asking for volunteers to translate or define them. Play a short game, if time allows, in which students create a sentence using one or more key words appropriately. Support vocabulary with visuals. Ask questions and ask for questions pertaining to the reading. Invite students to paraphrase and summarize what they have learned. This is helpful for all students.
- The sound of Hebrew might be new to many students. In using Hebrew vocabulary, pronounce words slowly, break them into syllables, and have students repeat each syllable, then whole words and phrases along with you and then after you.

  If you aren't a Hebrew teacher, feel free to ask a colleague to reinforce your Hebrew skills by practicing with you. There are websites that will pronounce words for you; select one that follows the Hebrew tradition of your congregation: Ashkenazic or Sephardic (modern Hebrew). Be aware of the reader's background as well. An Israeli's pronunciation will differ from an American's. Check with your education director as to the practice of the school. Your students will model your enthusiasm in using Hebrew.
- When students are asked to create a product of their learning, be open to students who find some vehicles challenging. Adapt a suggested task when needed. Allow for the student artist who has difficulty writing a paragraph, for the student who can create a song more successfully than a sentence, or the student who paints best with words.
- Reach out to your education director for suggestions and guidance. Follow the practice of your school in contacting parents regarding how you can help their child to be successful in your class.

Students are asked to master content and to demonstrate their knowledge of it. The Lesson Plan Manual offers suggestions to make those experiences successful for a variety of learners. Remember that a lesson plan is a recipe and that recipes can be altered. Add those elements that will allow for the best experiences for your learners.

CHAPTER

1 HIGHER THAN THE CLOUDS

Lesson 1

Essential Question: How is Israel the homeland of all Jews?

Lesson Objectives Students will be able to:

1. describe the difference between a home and a homeland.
2. list reasons that Israel is the Jewish homeland.
3. illustrate ways that Israel is *their* Jewish homeland.

Getting Started: (5 minutes)
On sheets of paper with the outline of a house, students answer the question, What makes a house a home? Conversation starters include: "In my house I have…"; "At their homes people…"; "At home I feel…" Record students' responses on the board or on a large sheet of paper under the heading, "What makes a house a home?"

Exploring the Text:

1. (10 minutes) A student reads aloud pages 5 and 6, then three volunteers, playing Daniel and his parents, act out the scene. Students list reasons that Israel is considered the Jewish homeland. Record responses on the board or a large sheet of paper titled, "What makes Israel the Jewish homeland?" Allow space for additions to the list in activity 2 below.
2. (15 minutes) Students complete **Imagine Israel** on page 7. To understand more about why some Jews move to Israel, have students read **Israel Is the Home of the Jewish People** on page 8 in *ḥevruta* (pairs or study partners). As they read, students underline additional reasons that Israel is considered the Jewish homeland. Add these reasons to the list begun in activity 1 above. Ask, How can a homeland feel close even when it is physically distant?
3. (5 minutes) A volunteer reads page 9. Using the **world map** on pages 10-11, students locate Israel and calculate its distance from their location. Students complete the exercise **How Big Is Israel?** on page 11 then brainstorm how Israel can be small and faraway, yet feel large and close to us. Compare and contrast the factors that make a home with those that make a homeland. Return to the scavenger hunt by reading pages 12-13.

Experiential Learning: (10 minutes)
Divided into pairs, students prepare to play the role of Daniel's parents, responding to Daniel's question on page 6, "How can it be like coming home again?"

Wrapping It Up: (5 minutes)
Using tracing paper, students trace the outline map of Israel on page 11, cut it out, and tape it onto the outline of the United States on page 10. How can a place that is so small feel so large?

The Tech Connection:
The Internet can enrich classroom learning. Go to http:/ / www. google.com / images or http:/ / www. bing.com / images to search for images of Israel.

Chapter 1: Lesson 2

Essential Question: In what ways is Israel a homeland?

Lesson Objectives Students will be able to:

1. explain how Israel is the homeland for a variety of Jews.
2. locate countries on a map from which Jews emigrated, such as Ethiopia, Russia, and Syria.
3. share information about the return of Ethiopian Jews to Israel.

Getting Started: (5 minutes)
Students suggest reasons that people might leave one country and move to another. *(People relocate to improve their lives. People are motivated by financial, personal, historical, and physical reasons.)*

Exploring the Text:

1. (5 minutes) As a class, students review in **Israel Is the Home of the Jewish People** (page 8) the freedoms Jews enjoy in Israel, highlighting the role of Israel as a land of refuge for people who were not permitted to live as Jews in the countries in which they were born.
2. (5 minutes) Using the **world map** on pages 10-11, children locate Russia, Syria, the United States, Canada, and England. (Note that Ethiopia is not visible on the map on page 11; you may wish to bring in a world map.) Ask, Which of these countries did Jews leave in order to be able to celebrate Jewish holidays, pray in a synagogue, and study Torah? In which countries can Jews do all of these things? Why do some Jews leave these countries anyway to move to Israel?
3. (15 minutes) Read a book to students or show a video about Operation Solomon (there are several on YouTube), the airlift that brought 14,000 Ethiopian Jews to Israel in 1991. Divide students into two groups, Ethiopian Jews arriving in Israel on Operation Solomon and Israelis welcoming them. Students in each group share their impressions. "Ethiopians" describe what it was like to fly on a plane for the first time and land in a modern country where no one spoke their language or knew their customs. "Israelis" explain how happy and proud they were to welcome the Ethiopian Jews home.

Experiential Learning: (10 minutes)
Sigd, once a holiday known only to Ethiopian Jews, is now a national holiday in Israel. Students can join in the celebration with music and dancing, and share Ethiopian food, such as Injera (the national bread), or a taste of honey, an ingredient in Ethiopian sweet bread. The delicious honey reminds us of the sweetness of freedom in our homeland Israel.

Wrapping It Up: (5 minutes)
Ask, What happens in a home when a new family member arrives? How is that reflected in Israel's welcome of their Ethiopian family?

The Tech Connection:
For information and photos, search online for "Operation Solomon," "Sigd," and "Injera" (or "Ethiopian Food"). http://www.youtube.com/ is a great source for videos about Operation Solomon and the Sigd observance.

Chapter 1: Lesson 3

Essential Question: What is Israel's neighborhood?

Lesson Objectives Students will be able to:

1. describe the function of a neighborhood.
2. list Israel's neighbors.
3. use the phrase *B'ruchim Haba'im* appropriately.

Getting Started: (10 minutes)
Students enter the classroom to find a long sheet of paper and markers in a central location. Students create a neighborhood, explaining the function of each of its parts (park—playing sports, exercise; library—borrowing books; firehouse—keeping us safe).

Exploring the Text:

1. (5 minutes) Turn to **The State of Israel map** on pages 14-15. Students are "Eretz Yisrael [Land of Israel] detectives." Who are Israel's neighbors? What do they notice about Israel's borders? About Israel's water sources and distribution? Conclude by looking at the symbols of the ancient land and the modern country of Israel on page 16. Tell students that they will learn about each one as the scavenger hunt unfolds.
2. (5 minutes) Turn to page 17. Examine the **photograph** for "evidence" that you couldn't be anywhere but Israel. Notice the sign that welcomes people from around the world to Israel. What sort of feeling does it create? How does it differ from a sign that just reads "Israel"?
3. (5 minutes) Students practice the phrase *b'ruchim haba'im*. Explain that the words *b'ruchim* and *b'rachah* share the same root. Each has to do with *blessing*. *B'ruchim haba'im* means, "blessed are those who enter." We say *b'ruchim haba'im* at the start of a Jewish wedding or baby naming ceremony, as well as when friends come to visit. How is it more than "hello"? When can we say *b'ruchim haba'im* in the classroom? *(when anyone enters the room)*

Experiential Learning: (15 minutes)
Download a map of the Middle East. Print one copy for each student on heavy paper. Students cut the map into a puzzle. Suggest a reasonable number of pieces, perhaps 6, to begin. Students put together their own puzzles then exchange puzzles with classmates. If time allows, have students cut the puzzle into 8 or 10 pieces to increase the degree of difficulty and the fun of the challenge. Store puzzles in plastic bags labeled with students' names to be used throughout the year as time allows.

Wrapping It Up: (5 minutes)
Students suggest why people and countries both need good neighbors.

The Tech Connection:
Download a version of the song "B'ruchim Haba'im" and play it softly as students work on their maps.

CHAPTER

2 HAIFA: The Busy Coast

Lesson 1

Essential Question: How can Hebrew be both an ancient and a modern language?

Lesson Objectives Students will be able to:

1. explain that languages are dynamic.
2. identify Eliezer Ben-Yehuda.
3. list some of the new Hebrew words they have learned.

Getting Started: (5 minutes)
Students enter the room to find modern objects, or pictures of objects, invented over the last 150 years (car, cell phone, computer, etc.). Students offer thoughts on what these items might have been called in 1492. Explain that languages grow as the world and technology change. People invent items and give them names. When Jews came from countries all over the world to settle in Palestine (now Israel) in the nineteenth century, they needed a way to communicate with each other and speak the language of the Jewish homeland, Hebrew, in their daily lives.

Exploring the Text:

1. (10 minutes) Students read pages 19-20. Volunteers dramatize the roles of Aunt Yael, Daniel, Rivkah, and Daniel's mother. Point out Eliezer Ben-Yehuda's **photo** on page 22. Students read **It's Not in the Torah** on page 21 in small groups and complete the activity individually. How long have Jews been speaking Hebrew? What do students notice about these Hebrew words? How do languages grow?
2. (10 minutes) Sing or play a recording or video of the songs "Hinei Mah Tov" and "Mah Tovu." Ask students to pick out the common word *tov*, "good." Teach that our use of *tov* begins in Genesis, when God looks at the world and remarks how *tov* it is. What are other ways we use the word *tov*? *(mazal tov, tov me'od, yom tov, tovah, lailah tov, erev tov, Shanah tovah)* List these words on the board along with their translations.
3. (10 minutes) Students work in *ḥevruta* (pairs) to create a short dialogue that includes a *tov* response. *(It's a special day. It's yom tov; Time to go to bed. Lailah tov.)* Pairs of students exchange dialogues, practicing other uses of *tov*.

Experiential Learning: (10 minutes)
Play the "Hebrew That We Already Know" game. The goals of the game are to demonstrate that students already know many Hebrew words and to reinforce vocabulary. Divide class into teams. Using pictures or objects, show the team that is up an item, or offer a clue about an item, and ask students to identify it, speaking only Hebrew. *(Examples: challah, kippah, menorah, bar/bat mitzvah, tallit, mezuzah, tzedakah, matzah, sukkah, Torah, yad, Aron Kodesh, Yisrael.)*

Wrapping It Up: (5 minutes)
Play a round of Word Whip with the words used in Experiential Learning. Each student is given a Hebrew word to translate into English as quickly as possible.

Chapter 2: Lesson 2

Essential Question: How can I imagine life in Haifa using all my senses?

Lesson Objectives Students will be able to:

1. locate Haifa on the map of Israel.
2. make comparisons about their life and life in Haifa.
3. explain the highlights of their Haifa experience.

Getting Started: (5 minutes)
Before class, list *hot dog, hamburger, falafel,* and *pizza* on the board. Create a mood by uploading Hebrew rock-and-roll music as background to the lesson. Using ballots or raising their hands, students vote for their favorite fast food. Show that all are available in Israel, using illustrations from the Internet or menus from Israeli restaurants, but that the order of preference might be different. Emphasize that this lesson will focus on how students' lives compare with life in Haifa.

Exploring the Text:

1. (10 minutes) Using their fingers, students trace the route along the coast from Tel Aviv (the airport) to Haifa on **The State of Israel map** on pages 14-15. A volunteer reads page 23. Looking at the **temperature chart** at the top of the page, students determine the areas of Israel that are the warmest, the city with the coolest temperature, and which city has the greatest temperature variation. Ask, Where in Israel would you like to spend your winter vacation? In advance, determine the average summer and winter temperatures in your locale. Students compare them to temperatures in Israeli cities. Students list what kind of clothing they would need to pack if they were visiting Haifa in the winter.
2. (10 minutes) Students familiarize themselves with the vocabulary in **A Window to Israel: Munchies** on page 24 then solve the **puzzle** on page 25. Two volunteers read **Let's Eat Out in Israel** on page 26. Students examine the restaurant sign for American influences. Ask: How does America influence Israeli food choices? How does Israel influence American food choices? (Advertisements for local stores can provide primary source materials.)
3. (10 minutes) If possible, purchase in advance Israeli imported food items, such as hummus, tehina, and falafel. (Be certain to check on student food allergies before finalizing the menu.) Students read the first two paragraphs on page 27 then close their books. Distribute *small* samples of Israeli food. It's time to eat! At the conclusion of their snack, students examine the packages. Where were the items made? How have they shared a taste of Israel?

Experiential Learning: (10 minutes)
Part of the fun of visiting a place is bringing home a souvenir. Students will create their own souvenirs of Haifa based on materials provided. Some possibilities include: mini clay falafel, magnets featuring Internet photos of Haifa, a miniscrapbook using original artwork.

Wrapping It Up: (5 minutes)
Students display their souvenirs and see what their classmates have done.

Chapter 2: Lesson 3

Essential Question: How is Haifa beautiful, enjoyable, and important?

Lesson Objectives Students will be able to:

1. explain the importance of ports to a country.
2. offer reasons for purchasing items from Israel.
3. share their impressions of Haifa.

Getting Started: (5 minutes)
Students brainstorm what a house needs to be a modern home. Ask: What does a country need to make it a thriving modern nation? List answers on the board. Suggest a seaport if nobody has mentioned this. Why is a port important for trade?

Exploring the Text:

1. (15 minutes) Open to page 27, third paragraph. Volunteers read pages 27-28. Ask, How many types of boats are mentioned? *(three: sailboats, ocean liners, and freighters)* Divide the class into three groups, one for each kind of boat. What does each type of boat mean to a country? *(fun, tourists, trade)* List student responses on the board. Each group designs a poster that advertises the importance of its type of boat to Israel. Students present posters and answer, What is Israel because it has Haifa? Display posters.
2. (5 minutes) Students complete **Time to Ship Off** on page 29. Ask: Why do people like to purchase items made in Israel?
3. (5 minutes) Read page 30 as a class. Partners fill in the words on the **Scavenger Hunt Sticker Stop** on page 31.

Experiential Learning: (15 minutes)
Students work in *ḥevruta* or small groups. Each group forms a consensus on the primary importance of buying Israeli items then designs a bumper sticker that advertises their perspective. Students in the group should create a slogan or symbol as part of their advertising campaign. Groups present their work.

Wrapping It Up: (5 minutes)
Each student offers one adjective to describe Haifa. Record them on a large sheet of paper labeled "Our Haifa." Display along with the posters and bumper stickers students have made.

CHAPTER

3 THE GALILEE: Rolling Through the North

Lesson 1

Essential Question: How is the Galilee a source of life for Israel?

Lesson Objectives Students will be able to:

1. trace the route from Haifa to Lake Kinneret on the map of Israel.
2. explain the importance of freshwater to Israel.
3. discuss the importance of trees and how trees are a gift.

Getting Started: (5 minutes)
Students close their eyes and imagine the land of Israel before the creation of people. They see trees, plants, and animals, but no buildings. Students open their eyes and share what they saw. Record responses in the center of a large sheet of paper for later use.

Exploring the Text:

1. (10 minutes) Students open the text to **The State of Israel map** on pages 14-15 and trace the path east from Haifa to Lake Kinneret. Turn to the **photo** on page 32. Students offer adjectives they would use to describe the landscape. Volunteers read pages 33-34. Ask, What kinds of trees grow in Israel besides olive trees? Why is it a mitzvah to grow trees? Read and complete **Plant a Tree of Your Own** on page 35.
2. (10 minutes) Ask, Why is water the source of life? Students study the **map of Northern Israel** on page 34, noting the shape of Lake Kinneret. Turn to page 36 for water facts, reading the first paragraph and **Israel Fun Fact.** What is the source of the water in Lake Kinneret, and what area of Israel does it go through? *(the most highly populated)* Students work in small groups as Committees to Protect the Kinneret and make their recommendations on protecting this critical water supply.
3. (15 minutes) Tell students that the Jewish people have been writing about trees from the time of the Torah until today. Recite the following verse by modern Israeli poet Nathan Zach:

   When is man like a tree of the field?
   Like the tree he thirsts for water.
   Like man he remains thirsty.
   And I do not know
   where I have been nor where I will be—
   like a tree of the field.

   Each student completes the following sentences on green, tree-shaped paper: *Like the tree of the field, I.... Like me, the tree of the field....*

Experiential Learning: (5 minutes)
Take out the list created in "Getting Started." Students paste their green trees around their initial impressions of Israel. Ask, What happens to Israel when we all plant trees?

Wrapping It Up: (5 minutes)
Brainstorm occasions when one might plant trees in Israel *(Tu BiShevat, Yom Ha'atzma'ut, when a baby is born, bar/bat mitzvah, birthday, any day!)*

The Tech Connection:
Visit the Jewish National Fund website for information and visuals on planting trees and water conservation in Israel.

Chapter 3: Lesson 2

Essential Question: In what ways is the Galilee unique from other regions of Israel?

Lesson Objectives Students will be able to:

1. locate Tiberias and Safed on the map of Israel.
2. describe the natural features of the Galilee.
3. list the unique experiences offered in the Galilee region.

Getting Started: (5 minutes)
As students enter the classroom, they are each given a list of places and features one might find in Israel. Students check off all items they believe can be found in Israel and put a question mark next to those items about which they are uncertain. (The list may include hot springs, snow, ski lift, fields of crops, mountains, and forests.) Students will return to their lists later on.

Exploring the Text:

1. (10 minutes) On **The State of Israel map** on pages 14-15 students locate Tiberias along the shore of Lake Kinneret. Remind students that Daniel and Rivkah were in the midst of their search for a water slide when we last met them. A volunteer reads the bottom two paragraphs of page 36. Ask, What's cool about hot springs? What is their source? Pairs of students read page 37. How many types of candles can students identify in **You're the Artist!** on page 38? *(birthday, Ḥanukkah, Havdalah)* What other types of candles do we light? *(Shabbat candles)* Students complete the activity on page 38.
2. (10 minutes) Students locate Safed on the **Northern Israel map** on page 34. Use pictures of Israeli artwork and crafts to illustrate one of the primary activities of Safed. Select art that contains Jewish images. Ask, What makes art Jewish? Highlight various techniques. Explain and show examples of mosaic art.
3. (5 minutes) Students travel east from Safed to the Golan Heights on the **Northern Israel map** on page 34. Ask, What are "heights"? Why are they strategically important? Partners read page 39. Ask, What are the surprises of the Galilee? What comes from the Golan Heights that is desperately needed in Israel? *(freshwater)*

Experiential Learning: (15 minutes)
Tearing or cutting small pieces of crepe paper, students glue them onto construction paper to create a mosaic depicting a natural feature (such as a fruit tree, snowy mountaintop, or hot springs) they discovered in the Galilee. Offer colors that emulate the colors of the mosaics they saw in the pictures shown above. Create a "Galilee Gallery" of their work.

Wrapping It Up: (5 minutes)
Students return to the lists generated in "Getting Started." Do they need to make any changes? Ask students to create pairs of contrasting words to explain the Galilee *(serious/fun, arty/sporty, hot/cold).*

Chapter 3: Lesson 3

Essential Question: What is daily life like for children in Israel?

Lesson Objectives Students will be able to:

1. articulate similarities and differences in the lives of school children in North America and Israel.
2. suggest places they would like to visit in the Galilee and offer reasons for their choices.
3. identify *Tzofim* and their similarities to and differences from North American scouting organizations.

Getting Started: (5 minutes)
On the board create four columns: School, Homework, After-school Activities, Watching TV / Playing Computer Games. As students enter the room, ask that they write in each column the *average* amount of time they spend on each activity every school day.

Exploring the Text:

1. (10 minutes) Tell students they will now compare their averages with those of an Israeli student. Small groups read **A Day in the Life of an Israeli Kid** on page 40 and review a typical day in the life of an Israeli child. Students individually complete their own schedules on page 41. Students compare their day with Rivkah's, circling those elements that are similar and underlining the major differences. List on the board the similarities and differences mentioned by students. (Remember that for Israeli students English is a foreign language!)
2. (10 minutes) A volunteer reads page 42. Students individually complete the **Scavenger Hunt Sticker Stop** on page 43. Think about all the fun and interesting places there are in the Galilee. Imagine that you spent a day there. Write a diary of your day. What did you do? What was the best part of the day? Students share their diary entries by reading them aloud.
3. (5 minutes) Ask students to return to page 41 and read the caption beneath the **photo** of the Israeli scouts, *Tzofim*. Note that the *Tzofim* was the first egalitarian scouting movement in the world. Based on what they know about Israeli school schedules, ask students why the *Tzofim* plays such an important role in the lives of Israeli children.

Experiential Learning: (15 minutes)
The motto of the *Tzofim*, like that of the Boy Scouts and Scouts Canada, is "Be Prepared." Scouts around the world earn badges for their accomplishments. Ask students to create a badge for themselves that shows how they are prepared for their "trip" to the Galilee. Students share their badge designs.

Wrapping It Up: (5 minutes)
Provide a banner on which you have written, "SURPRISE! It's the Galilee!" Write the word surprise in large bubble letters. Let students illustrate a Galilee surprise inside the word.

CHAPTER

4 TEL AVIV: The City That Never Sleeps

Lesson 1

Essential Question: Why is it fun to stay up late in Tel Aviv?

Lesson Objectives Students will be able to:

1. explain why Tel Aviv is called "The City That Never Sleeps."
2. compare and contrast Tel Aviv with their hometown.
3. consider the Galilee and Tel Aviv, and indicate where they would prefer to live.

Getting Started: (5 minutes)
Students list the pros and cons of visiting a place that is nothing like home and visiting a place that reminds them of home.

Exploring the Text:

1. (5 minutes) Compare and contrast the **photo** on page 44 with the **photo** on page 32. Volunteers suggest how each area compares with their hometown.
2. (10 minutes) Students turn to **The State of Israel map** on pages 14-15 and travel from Haifa to Tel Aviv. Why is it easy to find the way? What physical feature do they follow? *(the Mediterranean coastline)* Students imagine that they are going to Tel Aviv. Thumbing through the photos on pages 44-54, students write a list completing this sentence in as many ways as possible: "When I am in Tel Aviv, I will …." Students compare lists and explain why Tel Aviv is called "The City that Never Sleeps."
3. (10 minutes) Small groups read pages 45-46 and **Only in Israel** on page 47. Students complete the exercise on page 47, adding a star above anything they might also see in North America. Compare the similarities and differences between a mall in Israel and a mall in their hometown. A volunteer reads page 48 and the first paragraph on page 49. Students underline anything that is different from the town in which they live and put a star on those things that are the same. Log student responses on the board in two columns, "Same" and "Different."

Experiential Learning (15 minutes)
Divide class into two groups of designers. Each group designs a T-shirt to encourage Tel Aviv tourism. One group's theme is "Come to Tel Aviv….It's Just Like Home." The other group's theme is, "Come to Tel Aviv….It's Nothing Like Home." If there is time, each group should produce a banner, slogan, or jingle that supports their theme. Groups present their advertising campaigns to the class.

Wrapping It Up: (5 minutes)
Students vote on where they would prefer to live—in the Galilee or in Tel Aviv. Volunteers indicate on what basis they made their choice.

Chapter 4: Lesson 2

Essential Question: How does Israel show the world that it is a modern country?

Lesson Objectives Students will be able to:

1. give examples of Israel's contributions to modern science.
2. detail the experience of shopping in the *shuk*.
3. name their favorite places in Tel Aviv.

Getting Started: (10 minutes)
On the board, under the heading "What do they have in common?" write these words: *AOL Instant Messenger, camera pill, cell phone, Google, Grow Fish Anywhere, drip irrigation, solar power*. Explain that each is the product of an Israeli scientist or that Israel was a major contributor to the science that went into it. Explain less well-known items. Why is each important?

Exploring the Text:

1. (10 minutes) Students read page 49 silently and individually complete **A Window to Israel: Computers & Science** on page 50. Encourage students to think of a name for their robot that reflects its function. Students share inventions with the class.
2. (5 minutes) A volunteer reads the bottom left **photo** caption on page 51. Ask, What is the Hebrew word for *the computer*? Explain that the root of *hamaḥsheiv* is *ḥasheiv*, "think." Remind students of the work of Eliezer Ben-Yehuda, about whom they learned in chapter 2. In small groups students imagine they had the task of creating the single English word that became computer. Students share suggested names. Point to the **photo** of *Shuk Hacarmel* on page 51. Ask, Is Tel Aviv all high-tech? What do you think would be most fun about shopping at the *shuk*? What would be challenging about shopping there?
3. (10 minutes) In small groups students read page 52 and the bottom of page 53. Students individually complete the **Scavenger Hunt Sticker Stop** on page 53. A volunteer reads the first two paragraphs of page 54, then students plan a tour of Tel Aviv in **You Be the Tour Guide** on page 55. Survey students to determine which stops were the most popular.

Experiential Learning: (10 minutes)
Refer students to the **table-of-contents** (page 2). Ask, What are Daniel and Rivkah wearing? *(a kova tembel or Israeli sun hat, also called a "bucket hat")* Download and enlarge a picture of a *kova tembel*, or bring in a real one, and snap a photo of each student wearing it. Post student photos around the classroom. Students complete **Send a Postcard Home** on page 57 as they wait for their picture to be taken.

Wrapping It Up: (5 minutes)
Student volunteers offer "recollections" of their experiences in Tel Aviv.

The Tech Connection:
Search for "Israel technology" or by specific invention (e.g., "ReWalk") online.

Chapter 4: Lesson 3

Essential Question: What can we learn from Tel Aviv's name?

Lesson Objectives Students will be able to:

1. explain that the full name of the city is Tel Aviv-Jaffa.
2. translate the name Tel Aviv and explain the formation of an archaeological *tel*.
3. describe the life of Tel Aviv through the artifacts they've created for a *tel*.

Getting Started: (10 minutes)
Create a stack of newspapers, dated over a period of weeks, on a table. Arrange papers in chronological order, oldest at the bottom. Intersperse common items (or facsimiles) in the pile (e.g., package wrappers, a movie ticket, a bill, a half-eaten lollipop). Ask students to carefully dismantle the pile and determine when each item was left there. Have students log their findings. Explain that archaeologists engage in a similar process in trying to determine the age of items that are uncovered. They also learn information about how people lived then. Each of the mounds that archaeologists study is called a *tel* in Hebrew. Tel Aviv means "Hill of Spring."

Exploring the Text:

1. (5 minutes) A volunteer reads the bottom three paragraphs of page 54. Students turn to **Jaffa: The Oldest Port in the World** on page 56, examine the **photo** of Jaffa, and read the caption. Ask, How does the photo of Jaffa compare to the **photo** of Tel Aviv on page 44? What is unique about each place?
2. (10 minutes) Divide students into small groups. Assign each group a page (or pages) with photos or illustrations in chapter 4. Have each group determine the archaeological evidence that would be left by the activities shown or discussed on their assigned page(s). Each group creates a list of the items in their collection.
3. (10 minutes) Provide modeling clay or found objects (such as pottery shards, old coins, bits of wood, charcoal) for students to use to create the archaeological finds they've listed above. Each group will make a *tel*. Since the *tel* will depict the discards of a modern city, the "trash" will be quite similar to ours. Emphasize that archaeologists often find only small remnants of items, rather than whole objects, making it challenging to determine what activity a particular find may have been used for. (Items might be arranged in boxes of sand to simulate an archaeological dig.)

Experiential Learning: (10 minutes)
Students play archaeologists by visiting the *tel* items constructed by other groups and trying to determine the imagined source of each item.

Wrapping It Up: (10 minutes)
Tell about the *Tel*: Ask each student to be an archaeologist, explaining the items he or she created for the *tel*. Summarize life in Tel Aviv based on the items.

The Tech Connection:
Search engines such as http://www.google.com/images and www.http://bing.com/images can provide you with a wealth of Hebrew labels, maps, restaurant menus, and other "artifacts" of modern Israeli life. These would make great additions to the materials you provide.

CHAPTER

5 JERUSALEM: The Old and the New

Lesson 1

Essential Question: Why does Jerusalem have so many names?

Lesson Objectives Students will be able to:

1. cite four names for Jerusalem.
2. explain the significance of each of the selected names of Jerusalem.
3. propose a new name and symbol for Jerusalem based on their "visit" to the city.

Getting Started: (5 minutes)
Student volunteers share their names. What were they named by their parents? What are they called by their friends? By their siblings? By their grandparents? By their teammates? By their religious school teacher? Why are we called different names by different people? Explain that people—and places—are referred to by different names based on a variety of reasons. In this lesson students will learn four of Jerusalem's many names.

Exploring the Text:

1. (10 minutes) Turn to **The State of Israel** map on pages 14-15 and travel from Tel Aviv to Jerusalem. A volunteer reads page 59. Students derive one of Jerusalem's names from the reading. *(Jerusalem of Gold)* Pairs of students read pages 60-63. Challenge students to discover three more of Jerusalem's names as they work together. *(the Holy City, City of David, City of Peace)* Post names on the board.
2. (15 minutes) Parts of Jerusalem have names, too. There is the New City and the Old City. Students individually review pages 58-63, marking those elements that they think are new with an *N* (cars, street lights, Knesset) and those that they think are old with an *O (city walls, menorah, donkey as transportation)*. Share and compare. Emphasize that ancient and modern live side by side in Israel.

Experiential Learning: (15 minutes)
The names of Jerusalem reflect different aspects of the city. Divide students into small groups. Each group gives Jerusalem a new name based on their learning experiences. Students create a symbol for Jerusalem based on their new name. Each group shares with the class their name and symbol.

Wrapping It Up: (5 minutes)
Volunteers select one of Jerusalem's four names and offer a reason that Jerusalem was given that name. *(appearance, religious feeling, history, hope)*

The Tech Connection:
Virtual tours of many of the world's cities are available online. They can be living bulletin boards that create an engaging classroom atmosphere. Search for "Jerusalem virtual tour" in any search engine.

Chapter 5: Lesson 2

Essential Question: How can we work for peace in Jerusalem?

Lesson Objectives Students will be able to:

1. explain why Jerusalem is called the "City of Peace."
2. cite factors that enable people of different backgrounds to coexist.
3. translate the word *peace* into Hebrew and Arabic.

Getting Started: (5 minutes)
Each student is given a page with *Yerushalayim,* the Hebrew name for Jerusalem, written at the top in Hebrew letters. On the board write the word *shalom* (peace) in Hebrew letters. Provide markers or crayons, and ask students to find and outline the letters that spell *shalom* in *Yerushalayim (the root shin-lamed-mem).* How does the name "City of Peace" reflect our feelings about peace?

Exploring the Text:

1. (10 minutes) Students turn to **Seeking Peace** on page 64. Emphasize that peace is not just a goal for countries, but for individuals as well. Peace is an important goal for the classroom, and creating rules that everyone values can help the class achieve peace. Working in small groups, students complete the exercise on page 64. Students share responses and reach consensus on five rules for the class. Post those rules on a large sheet of paper/poster board.
2. (10 minutes) Students read **A Window to Israel: Working for Peace** on page 65 and complete the first question individually. Answers to question 1 are shared in small groups. These groups complete question 2. Groups share responses with class. *(Answers may include, We can get to know people of different religions.)*
3. (10 minutes) Using examples from students' experiences, remind them that Jews pray for peace; that we call our most holy city, Jerusalem, the "City of Peace"; and that we sing about peace. Teach a prayer for peace in Hebrew and Arabic by learning the song "Od Yavo Shalom Aleinu" (peace will come to us). Its refrain is sung in Hebrew and Arabic (shalom/salaam). Invite the rabbi or cantor to teach this song to your class, or find the music online at YouTube. The words are:

Od yavo shalom aleinu	Peace will come upon us
Od yavo shalom aleinu	Peace will come upon us
Od yavo shalom aleinu	Peace will come upon us
Ve'al kulam (x2)	And on everyone
Salaam	Salaam ["peace" in Arabic]
Aleinu ve'al kol ha'olam,	On us and on everyone
Salaam, Salaam (x2)	Salaam, Salaam

Experiential Learning: (10 minutes)
Search the Internet for sites that offer English-Arabic and English-Hebrew translations. Look up *salaam,* the Arabic word for "peace," and *shalom,* the Hebrew word for "peace." Select a simple font. Enlarge the words as desired. Using opaque paper and brush markers, have students copy the words *salaam* and *shalom* to create wall hangings for their homes.

Wrapping It Up: (5 minutes)
Students share ways they can learn about different faiths: talking to parents, library books, existing community initiatives, inviting guests to class.

Chapter 5: Lesson 3

Essential Question: Why is Jerusalem the Jewish Holy City?

Lesson Objectives Students will be able to:

1. identify the *Kotel* and cite aspects of its history.
2. define holiness and explain the *Kotel* as the holiest site in the Jewish world.
3. explain the tradition of placing notes of prayer in the *Kotel*.

Getting Started: (5 minutes)
Write the question, "What does *holy* mean?" on the blackboard. Students write their answers on paper. Create a collective definition and write it on the board.

Exploring the Text:

1. (15 minutes) Volunteers read pages 66-67. The most holy Jewish site in the world—the *Kotel*—is a 2,000-year-old retaining wall. Give each student a sheet of paper on which is an illlustration of a stone in the Wall, and ask them to indicate what they believe makes the *Kotel* holy. Students share responses and assemble their stones together as a bulletin board, creating a word picture of the holiness of the *Kotel*.
2. (15 minutes) Explain that some people go to the *Kotel* to sightsee, while others gather at the *Kotel* to pray. Some visitors tuck written prayers between the stones of the *Kotel*. Ask students, Why do people pray? *(Responses might include, to "talk" to God, to feel better, to be with other people.)* Write each response on a separate sheet of paper. Mount each sheet in a different location around the room. Ask students to go to the sign that best answers the question for them. At each location students should discuss their feelings with others who share them. One spokesperson from each group should share their group's answers with the class.
3. (10 minutes) Students complete **Write a Note to God** on page 68 and the **Scavenger Hunt Sticker Stop** on page 69, and copy their prayers onto small pieces of paper.

Experiential Learning: (5 minutes)
Students approach the *Kotel* they created in Activity 1 and insert their prayers.

Wrapping It Up: (5 minutes)
Student volunteers respond to the question, Why would you like to visit the *Kotel*?

The Tech Connection:
If your classroom has Internet access, view the live *Kotel* cam.

CHAPTER

6 THE JUDEAN DESERT AND NEGEV: It's a Heat Wave

Lesson 1

Essential Question: What are the unique historical and physical features of the Negev?

Lesson Objectives Students will be able to:

1. locate the Negev and Beersheva on the map of Israel.
2. offer an abbreviated history of Masada.
3. explain how the Dead Sea can be both dead and alive.

Getting Started: (5 minutes)
Explain that this lesson begins with the story of Jews protecting Judaism against the Romans, who did not want the Jews to practice their faith. Ask, How do you protect something that is important to you?

Exploring the Text:

1. (10 minutes) Students turn to **The State of Israel map** on pages 14-15 and trace the route south from Jerusalem to the Negev. A volunteer reads page 71 and the first sentence on page 72. In order to save Judaism, some Jews fled to the Negev to hide from the Romans. Looking at the **photo** on page 72, students offer their perspectives on why Masada seemed a safe place to practice Judaism undisturbed. (A general statement about the siege of Masada is appropriate for this age group: The siege ultimately ended with the suicide of its Jewish defenders, who chose death over capture by the Romans.)
2. (10 minutes) In *ḥevruta*, students read pages 72-73. How did the Dead Sea get its name? How is it very much alive? Students locate Beersheva on **The State of Israel map** on pages 14-15 and read pages 74 and 77. Referring to the map, students look at the distance that water must travel to get to Beersheva. What must everyone remember in Beersheva? Students individually complete **Be a Pen Pal** on page 75, sharing their questions and answers in small groups. (Please note that "Hatikvah" is covered in lesson 2. Do not read A Hopeful People on page 75 until the next lesson.)
3. (10 minutes) In small groups students list contrasting pairs of adjectives to describe the Judean desert. *(e.g., dry/cultivated)* Once they've completed their lists, use them to play an elimination game. Each group takes turns offering one pair of adjectives. All teams with that pair cross it off their list. The team with the last pair of unique adjectives wins.

Experiential Learning: (10 minutes)
Show a photo of a person reading while floating in the Dead Sea. To understand the feeling of saltwater in the Dead Sea, pairs of students dissolve 4 tablespoons of salt into 2 cups of water. Advanced Experiment: Fill a glass half full of saltwater according to the above recipe. Slowly add plain water by pouring it down the side of the glass, being careful not to mix the regular water into the saltwater. Gently drop a raw egg into the water and watch as it sinks through the plain water and stops when it hits the saltwater.

Wrapping It Up: (5 minutes)
Student volunteers respond to the question, What is amazing about the desert area of Israel?

Chapter 6: Lesson 2

Essential Question: What is "Hatikvah"—the song and the hope?

Lesson Objectives Students will be able to:

1. define the word *hatikvah* and identify "Hatikvah" as Israel's national anthem.
2. express the aspirations of "Hatikvah."
3. list hopes Jews have today.

Getting Started: (5 minutes)
If possible, play a loop of "Hatikvah" in the background. Distribute copies of the "Star-Spangled Banner," telling students that national anthems often mention what people hope for. Ask students to underline the expressions of hope they find in the "Star-Spangled Banner" and share their answers with the class. Explain that the national anthem of Israel is called "Hatikvah," which means "The Hope."

Exploring the Text:

1. (5 minutes) A volunteer reads **A Hopeful People** on page 75. Ask, For how many years have people been singing "Hatikvah" in the State of Israel?
2. (10 minutes) Tell students that "Hatikvah" was written in Europe long before Israel became an independent nation. Divide the class into small groups, distributing copies of "Hatikvah" and four (different) colored highlighters or pencils to each group. Explain that "Zion" is another name for Israel. Ask, What hope is expressed in "Hatikvah"? What kept our hope for Israel alive? For how long has this been our dream? In which direction is the land of Israel for most Jews? Groups highlight or underline the answer to each question in a different color.
3. (10 minutes) "Hatikvah" expresses the Jewish longing to be a free people in their own land. That wish came true in 1948, yet Israelis continue to sing the same song. Why? "Hatikvah" is sung not only in Israel but when Jews gather all over the world. Why? Students share their hopes for Israel. Using any of the audio versions available, begin singing "Hatikvah" with the class. As time permits during future lessons, continue this activity.

Experiential Learning: (15 minutes)
Explain the tradition of marking the eastern wall in Jewish homes and praying while facing east, *mizraḥ*. If we are always reminded of the direction, what do we remember? *(Israel/Jerusalem)* Using a selection of materials, students make a *mizraḥ* to hang on an eastern wall in their school or classroom. Write the word *mizraḥ* in Hebrew letters on banner paper, dividing each letter into sections. Students work in small groups to complete each section.

Wrapping It Up: (5 minutes)
Remind students that Jews hoped for a land for 2,000 years. Have students share their thoughts about the importance of hope.

Chapter 6: Lesson 3

Essential Question: What is unique about kibbutz life?

Lesson Objectives Students will be able to:

1. explain the origin of the kibbutz.
2. discuss how *kibbutzim* make decisions.
3. debate the positives and negatives of kibbutz life.

Getting Started: (10 minutes)
Working in small groups, students are asked to imagine that they are in charge of cleaning, painting, and redecorating their classroom. How would they determine who should help with each job? What if there was a job no one wanted? What if someone was unable to work? Tell students that they have just worked cooperatively to solve a community problem, with each person contributing to the answer. This lesson will look at a way this was done in Israel.

Exploring the Text:

1. (15 minutes) A volunteer reads the caption for the top **photo** on page 76. Explain that when Kibbutz Deganyah was established in 1910, the land of Israel had been neglected for a long time. Some areas of Israel were very dry; others were swampy and bug infested. Settlers came from Europe, where they had had no farming experience and were faced with having to build homes, feed their families, and care for their children with no outside help. Students work in small groups devising solutions to how to begin settling the land. Groups share their responses. Write those ideas that fit the description of a kibbutz on the board. Conclude by emphasizing the importance of people working together to solve a common problem. You might cite an accomplishment achieved by your school or congregation coming together with a common purpose.
2. (10 minutes) A volunteer reads **A Window to Israel: Kibbutzim** on page 76. Students complete the exercise individually. In the early years of kibbutz life, all children on the kibbutz often slept together in special buildings, cared for by designated adults. Having care givers for the children allowed more adults to work in the fields. Divide the class into two groups, one supporting the practice of children sleeping away from their parents, the other opposing it. Students debate the merits of each.
3. (5 minutes) Students read and complete **The Negev Packing List** on page 78 and the **Scavenger Hunt Sticker Stop** on page 79. Students look back at page 39. What piece of equipment in the drawing on page 78 would come in handy in the Golan Heights?

Experiential Learning: (5 minutes)
Kibbutzim are democracies in which the residents make all policy decisions. Students cast secret ballots supporting or opposing children sleeping in a separate building from their parents. Votes are tallied.

Wrapping It Up: (5 minutes)
Students volunteer what they think would be most fun about living on a kibbutz.

The Tech Connection:
Search for the term "kibbutz" on http://www.google.com/images for pictures for your classroom.

CHAPTER

7 EILAT: Snorkeling in the Red Sea

Lesson 1

Essential Question: What can we learn about Shabbat from Daniel and Rivkah's Eilat Shabbat?

Lesson Objectives Students will be able to:

1. locate Eilat on the map of Israel and describe its unique location.
2. translate the phrase and explain the concept of *Shabbat shalom.*
3. cite examples of Shabbat activities and create a personal vision of Shabbat from among them.

Getting Started: (5 minutes)
If students have learned Hebrew holiday vocabulary, ask, What holiday greetings do Jews share with one another? *(Shana Tovah—Happy New Year, yom huledet same'aḥ—happy birthday, ḥag same'aḥ—happy holiday)* If not, begin by telling students that Jews have many traditional greetings and cite examples. Ask, If *Shabbat* means "the Sabbath," and *shalom* means "peace," what do we mean when we say *Shabbat shalom*? List responses on the board. Tell students that their trip to Eilat will help them understand what *Shabbat shalom* might mean.

Exploring the Text:

1. (5 minutes) Students turn to **The State of Israel map** on pages 14-15 and travel south to Eilat, making observations about Eilat's unique location. Students turn to the **photo** on page 80 and comment on Eilat's physical features. Note the proximity of the desert to the water. Ask, Why are there direct flights from Europe to Eilat?
2. (15 minutes) In small groups, students read pages 81-82, underlining all the preparations that are being made for Shabbat. Students share responses. Ask each student to select two practices from the list that they would like to try. *(Examples include buying flowers and eating ḥallah.)* Emphasize that some practices are rituals (such as lighting candles) and others are personal (wearing nice clothes, eating special foods, being with family and friends). Students turn to **You're the Artist** on page 83 and create a stamp that illustrates their idea of a wonderful Shabbat.
3. (10 minutes) A volunteer reads page 84. Pairs of students play the game **A Lot in Eilat** on page 85.

Experiential Learning: (10 minutes)
Each student or pair of students selects a favorite Eilat activity (observing fish, parasailing) and pantomimes it. Other students guess the activity being portrayed.

Wrapping It Up: (5 minutes)
Volunteers explain how the Shabbat activities they chose can contribute to bringing about *Shabbat shalom.* Encourage students who selected activities that may be regarded as non-traditional, such as going to the beach, to explain why they, too, increase *Shabbat shalom.*

Chapter 7: Lesson 2

Essential Question: How can we play like Israelis?

Lesson Objectives Students will be able to:

1. describe and demonstrate selected Israeli games.
2. explain that some children's games are common to Israel and America.
3. use simple Hebrew vocabulary in playing selected games.

Getting Started: (5 minutes)
Students suggest differences and similarities between their lives and those of Israeli children. Sort answers on board in two separate columns. Remind students that all children enjoy playing games. Sometimes those games are familiar, and sometimes they are new. Today's lesson will be all play—Israeli-style!

Exploring the Text: (30 minutes)
Use a round-robin format, dividing total class time by the number of games you choose to play.

Activity 1
Students read page 86 and **A Window to Israel: Sports Crazy** on page 87. *Matkot* means "rackets" or "paddles." Some say it is the Israeli national game! It has no rules and requires no net or court. It's "Smashball" in the United States, usually played with imported Israeli equipment. Find directions and YouTube videos on line. Students can create the challenge indoors using balled up paper or foil and their hand as a paddle.

Activity 2
Tell students that marbles are all the rage in Israeli schools, but to play like an Israeli child, they need to play in Hebrew. A marble is a *goolah* (pl. *goolot*). A red marble is a *ketchupia*. A blue-and-white marble is a *Yisra'elit*. Ask, where do these names come from? Find various Israeli marble terms and games online.

Activity 3
Create Hebrew tongue twisters or find them online (with transliteration). Set time limits or use a timer to raise the degree of difficulty.

Activity 4
Ḥameish Avanim, Five Stones, is Jacks played Israeli-style. Instructions can be found online. Sugar cubes or small stones are perfect substitutes for the *kugelach,* little metal blocks, that are the "official" equipment. Provide vocabulary sheets with numbers in Hebrew to be used during the game.

Activity 5 (Optional activity for the class)
Israelis play American games. Provide materials from the Jewish National Fund about "Project Baseball," and learn how JNF is helping Israeli children play the American game. Consider the possibility of supporting the project with tzedakah money.

Experiential Learning: (10 minutes)
American children can turn the American pastime into Hebrew practice by creating a banner with the name of their favorite baseball team—spelled phonetically in Hebrew. Examples can be found on sites that offer Hebrew T-shirts and baseball caps.

Wrapping It Up: (5 minutes)
Students brainstorm how they can add Hebrew to their favorite American games.

CHAPTER 7: Lesson 3

Essential Question: What is a desert?

Lesson Objectives Students will be able to:

1. explain the uniqueness of the palm tree and its fruit.
2. suggest why Israel is called the "Land of Milk and Honey."
3. illustrate desert life in art.

Getting Started: (5 minutes)
Students complete the sentence, "A desert is…." Responses are listed on the board.

Exploring the Text:

1. (5 minutes) Students read page 88 and review Eilat's location at the southern tip of the Negev on the **Israel Locator** on page 81. Looking back at the pictures in chapter 7, students observe the roles played by palm trees *(shade, beautification)*. Ask, On what holiday do we use palm branches? *(On Sukkot, for the lulav).* Why do their thick trunks and many leaves make palm trees suited for the desert?
2. (15 minutes) Students compile a list of fruit trees. Add date palm if not included on the class list. In the Torah, Israel is called the "Land of Milk and Honey," but the honey does not come from bees. It comes from trees! Taste dates and figs, using fresh and dried fruits. What makes them perfect desert fruits? Compare their flesh with thinner-skinned fruits. Find a date honey recipe and partially prepare in advance; some dates will require about an hour to boil. Students complete the preparation of the honey by mashing the dates then sampling. They might also create a syrup by adding water to the honey. Try adding cinnamon, too. Have small containers available so that students can share the sweet treat with their families.

Experiential Learning: (20 minutes)
In 2006 Israel issued a series of stamps called "The Children of America Paint Israel." Images are available online. Students are asked to "paint the desert" the way they have experienced it. (Explain that painting an impression is different than painting a realistic scene.) What impressions do students have of the Israeli desert? Students might look over chapters 6 and 7 for inspiration. Each picture could serve as a segment of a larger mural.

Wrapping It Up: (10 minutes)
Student artists exhibit their work and explain their selection of desert images. Have students compare their art with their description of a desert at the start of the lesson. What, if anything, has changed? Create a gallery entitled "Our Class Paints the Desert."

CHAPTER

8 HOME

Lesson 1

Essential Question: How do we show that we are *ḥaveirim*, "friends"?

Lesson Objectives Students will be able to:

1. define and appropriately use friend-related vocabulary.
2. compare and contrast personal friendship with being a friend of Israel.
3. articulate ways they can be friends to Israel.

Getting Started: (5 minutes)
Ask, Why is it difficult to say good-bye to a friend? Why is it better to say "see you again"? Student volunteers act out leaving a relative or friend using each ending. How are they different?

Exploring the Text:

1. (10 minutes) A volunteer reads page 91. A friend who is a boy is a *ḥaveir*. A friend who is a girl is a *ḥaveirah*. Several friends are *ḥaveirim* (masculine)/*ḥaveirot* (feminine). Write the words on the board. Students identify themselves as a *ḥaveir* or a *ḥaveirah* and form groups of *ḥaveirim* (all male or mixed-gender groups) or *ḥaveirot* (all female groups). Volunteers say good-bye to a female friend, a male friend, and several friends. Play or sing the words of "Shalom Ḥaveirim." Remind students that they already know all the words of the song except one, *l'hitra'ot*, which means "see you again." Sing the song as a class.
2. (15 minutes) Students are reminded of the welcome they received at the airport when they arrived in Israel (page 17). We greet visitors to our homes in the same way: *b'ruchim haba'im.* Using clear plastic plates, students create a serving tray to use at home to welcome guests. Between the plates they glue a decorative *b'ruchim habaim*, using a preprinted version of the words that they embellish with markers.
3. (5 minutes) In what ways is loving a relative or friend like loving Israel? In what ways is it different? Must one love everything about a person or place? How should people treat one another all the time? *(respect one another, share their ideas, care for one another)* Students complete **Loving Israel** on page 92.

Experiential Learning: (10 minutes)
Using plastic wristbands (available at craft shops) and markers, students write "I ♥ Israel's…." *(people, beaches, coral reefs, Kotel, games).*

Wrapping It Up: (5 minutes)
Students model their bracelets and offer ways that they will be friends to Israel.

Chapter 8: Lesson 2

Essential Question: What are you bringing home from Israel and how are you carrying it with you?

Lesson Objectives Students will be able to:

1. describe a variety of ways in which we carry things with us.
2. cite ways they are bringing home memories of Israel.
3. share a memory they are bringing home from Israel.

Getting Started: (5 minutes)
On individual slips of paper, one per idea, each student contributes responses to the question, In what ways do we carry things with us? *(in our luggage, in our memories)*

Exploring the Text:

1. (5 minutes) Students read and complete pages 93-94 and the **Scavenger Hunt Sticker Stop** on page 95.
2. (5 minutes) Students sort the responses from "Getting Started" into categories:
   a. using our hands
   b. using our heads *(things we remember)*
   c. using our hearts *(what we feel)*
   d. other

   Can we see everything we carry with us? How do we make memories we can't see real? *(Memories lead to behaviors; we do things because we remember. We might eat falafel at home; we might tell others about our experiences.)*
3. (20 minutes) Students working in *ḥevruta* outline one another on life-size sheets of paper. Students personalize their outlines by dressing them in ways that are appropriate to activities that might be performed in Israel. *(swimming, skiing, going on a dig)* They share the Israel memories portrayed in their drawings and indicate near the appropriate physical area on their drawing what they will be bringing home from Israel. Students include items that are visible and those that are carried in their hearts and minds. Students might be provided with bags that can be filled with souvenirs they create, which they attach to their figures. Join figures to create a display around the room or in the hallway.

Experiential Learning: (15 minutes)
Students write rhyming couplets. *(Jerusalem, the City of Gold / Part of it's new and part of it's old; Tel Aviv, sand and sea / lots of fun for you and me)*

Wrapping It Up: (5 minutes)
Poems are shared and saved to be used in the concluding lesson.

Chapter 8: Lesson 3 *Concluding Special Event*

Essential Question: How can we preserve and share our memories of Israel?

Lesson Objectives Students will be able to:

1. share ways that we can evoke memories.
2. create a series of books as memory albums that serve to illustrate and explain their Israel experience.

Preparation:

In this concluding activity, students will create an Israel album in the form of a "lap book," a series of small books featuring their choice of Israel memories, which are mounted onto one backing board or file folder. Instructions for a variety of easy-to-prepare minibooks can be found in craft guides or online. Advance preparation of an assortment of small books is recommended. Parents, teen aides, or seniors in the community might be willing to help. Many require only paper folding or assembly with a single staple. While minibooks are simple, their diversity is engaging. Search for a variety of styles and shapes (folding one page into a book, one that opens like a matchbook) Prepared books allow students to devote their time to creating content.

Getting Started:

Students think of a picture of themselves that is several years old. Ask, What does it remind you of, even if it isn't obvious to somebody else looking at the picture? Students share descriptions of their photos and the memories they evoke. A volunteer reads the first two paragraphs on page 93.

Activity:

Each student will create a series (perhaps 4-5) of small albums (approximately 3 x 3 inches or 2 x 4 inches), each summarizing an aspect of their Israel experience.

Topics:

Teacher might assign certain topics or students might choose their own. Possibilities include: individual cities, bodies of water, topography, regions of Israel, foods of Israel, adventures and activities, My Jewish Homeland, land of contrasts.

Contents of books:

Each book should have a title describing its contents. The number of pages of each book and content requirements are dependent upon teacher and students.

Assembling the lap book:

Student-made books are glued to backing, with any stickers or decorative trim that is available. The poem created in the previous lesson would make a suitable feature of the lap book.

Wrapping It Up:

Parents might be invited for the last 5 minutes of class for the presentation of **Israel Certificates of Achievement** (page 96) and the sharing of lap books.

Assessments

Student learning is assessed through participation in projects, contribution to class discussions, and individual work.

Assessing mastery of *The Great Israel Scavenger Hunt* might include:

- Do students demonstrate familiarity with the map of Israel?
- Do students use the names of specific cities and geographical features in describing Israel?
- Does student conversation and play reflect excitement about Israel and the concepts and vocabulary taught?
- Do students demonstrate positive attitudes toward their learning? Are they proud of their work?

The open-ended questions below are designed to have students reflect on their personal understanding of the concepts taught in each chapter. You may choose to adapt or create your own questions.

Chapter 1

1. Many things are important to people; in what ways can a country be important to a person?
2. Many things make us feel welcome; in what ways do we feel welcome in a place?

Chapter 2

1. Like people, places have a "face" that others see. What faces does Israel show the world?
2. Where a person lives matters. How does its location matter to Israel?

Chapter 3

1. A country lives on its land. What do the people of Israel have to do to live on their land?
2. How do Israelis enjoy their land?

Chapter 4

1. If cities could tell stories about the people who live in them, what would Tel Aviv say about the people who live there?
2. If you took a picture of Tel Aviv, what would it show and teach about the city?

Chapter 5

1. Some cities live in different times all at the same time. How does Jerusalem live in all times all at once?
2. Like people, each city has a personality. What is Jerusalem's personality?

Chapter 6

1. Nature gives us challenges and gifts. How does Israel use the gifts of the desert?
2. How does Israel meet the challenges of the desert?

Chapter 7

1. Eilat wants to have fun. How does its location make it fun?
2. Eilat is a wonderful place to experience the shalom of Shabbat. How would you and your family share a *Shabbat shalom*, a Sabbath of peace?

Chapter 8

1. People sometimes say that "Home is where the heart is." How can parts of your heart be in different places?
2. When do you want to visit Israel, and how will you keep Israel close until you do?